PILOT
LEVEL 3

PAPER AIRPLANES

BY CHRISTOPHER L. HARBO

CAPSTONE PRESS
a capstone imprint

TABLE OF

contents

prepare for TakeOFF

Welcome aboard! You've earned the rank of pilot and you're ready to fly. Now it's time to prepare eight planes for takeoff. Are you up to the challenge? Strap yourself into the pilot's seat and let's find out.

LeveL 3

As pilot, your first duty is to polish your paper folding skills. The instructions for these models will test you, but never give up. Read each step carefully and take your time. With patience and practice, you'll have these planes streaking across the schoolyard.

materials

Every paper airplane builder needs a well-stocked toolbox. The models in this book use the materials listed below. Take a minute before you begin folding to gather what you need:

 **paper** Any paper you can fold will work. Notebook paper is always popular. But paper with cool colors and designs gives your planes style.

 **scissors** Keep a scissors handy. Some models need a snip here or there to fly well.

 Rubber bands Rubber bands can send some airplane models sailing. Long, thin rubber bands work well.

 paper clips Paper clips are perfect for adding weight to a plane's nose. Keep a supply of small and large paper clips on hand.

 **small binder clips** Small binder clips also give weight to a glider's nose.

Techniques and Terms

Folding paper airplanes isn't difficult when you understand common folding techniques and terms. Review this list before folding the models in this book. Remember to refer back to this list if you get stuck on a tricky step.

Valley Folds

Valley folds are represented by a dashed line. The paper is creased along the line. The top surface of the paper is folded against itself like a book.

Mountain Folds

Mountain folds are represented by a pink or white dashed and dotted line. The paper is creased along the line and folded behind.

Reverse Folds

Reverse folds are made by opening a pocket slightly and folding the model inside itself along existing creases.

Mark
FOLDS

Mark folds are light folds used to make reference creases for a later step. Ideally, a mark fold will not be seen in the finished model.

RABBIT
ear
FOLDS

Rabbit ear folds are formed by bringing two edges of a point together using existing creases. The new point is folded to one side.

SQUASH
FOLDS

Squash folds are formed by lifting one edge of a pocket and reforming it so the spine gets flattened. The existing creases become new edges.

FOLDING SYMBOLS

Fold the paper in the direction of the arrow.

Fold the paper behind.

Fold the paper and then unfold it.

Turn the paper over or rotate it to a new position.

A fold or edge hidden under another layer of paper; also used to mark where to cut with a scissors

LIFTOFF

DESIGNED BY CHRISTOPHER L. HARBO

Ever wish you could put more power behind your launch? Your wish is granted with this plane. The notch in Liftoff's nose is strong enough to withstand the pull of a rubber band. Get ready. Aim. Fire away!

materials

* 8.5- by 11-inch (22- by 28-centimeter) paper
* scissors
* rubber band

start Here

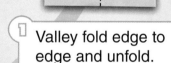

1 Valley fold edge to edge and unfold.

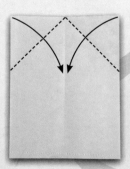

2 Valley fold the corners to the center.

3 Mountain fold the point.

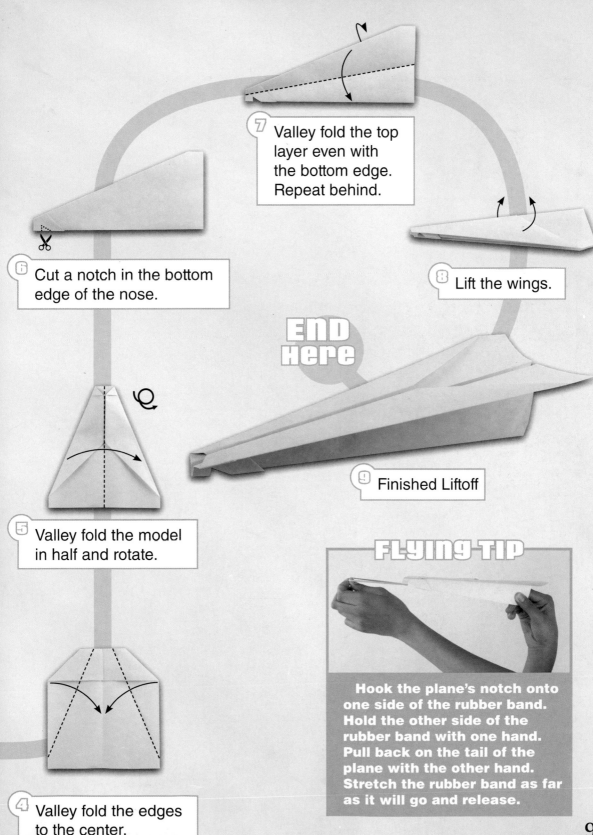

7 Valley fold the top layer even with the bottom edge. Repeat behind.

6 Cut a notch in the bottom edge of the nose.

8 Lift the wings.

END HERE

5 Valley fold the model in half and rotate.

9 Finished Liftoff

FLYING TIP

Hook the plane's notch onto one side of the rubber band. Hold the other side of the rubber band with one hand. Pull back on the tail of the plane with the other hand. Stretch the rubber band as far as it will go and release.

4 Valley fold the edges to the center.

NEEDLE NOSE

TRADITIONAL MODEL

It's not hard to figure out how the Needle Nose got its name. This model's pointy beak gets damaged easily. But the plane's awesome flights will make up for the time you spend straightening the nose.

MATERIALS

• 8.5- by 11-inch (22- by 28-cm) paper

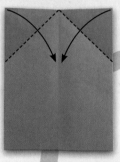

Start Here

1 Valley fold edge to edge and unfold.

2 Valley fold the corners to the center.

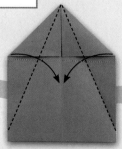

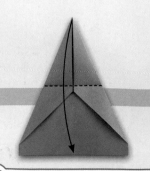

3 Valley fold the edges to the center.

4 Valley fold the point.

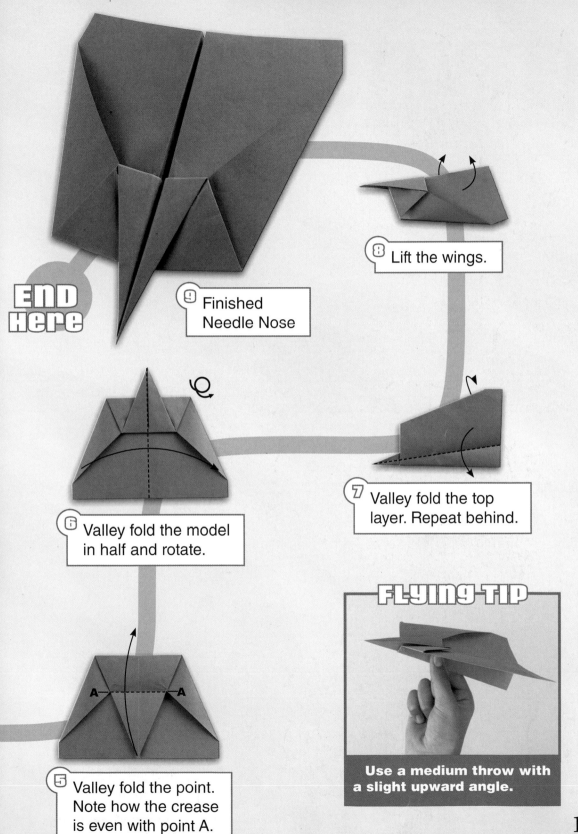

END HERE

⑨ Finished Needle Nose

⑧ Lift the wings.

⑥ Valley fold the model in half and rotate.

⑦ Valley fold the top layer. Repeat behind.

FLYING TIP

⑤ Valley fold the point. Note how the crease is even with point A.

A———A

Use a medium throw with a slight upward angle.

AVIATOR

TRADITIONAL MODEL

The Aviator is one cool mini jet. This model looks like a dart and has a built-in cockpit. With a strong throw, you might think a tiny pilot is guiding it across the room.

materials

* 6-inch (15-cm) square of paper

8 Pull up the triangle in the nose to form a cockpit.

9 Lift the wings.

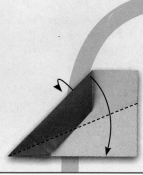

7 Valley fold the top layer even with the bottom edge. Repeat behind.

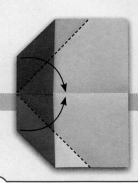

6 Mountain fold the model in half.

5 Valley fold the edges to the center.

12

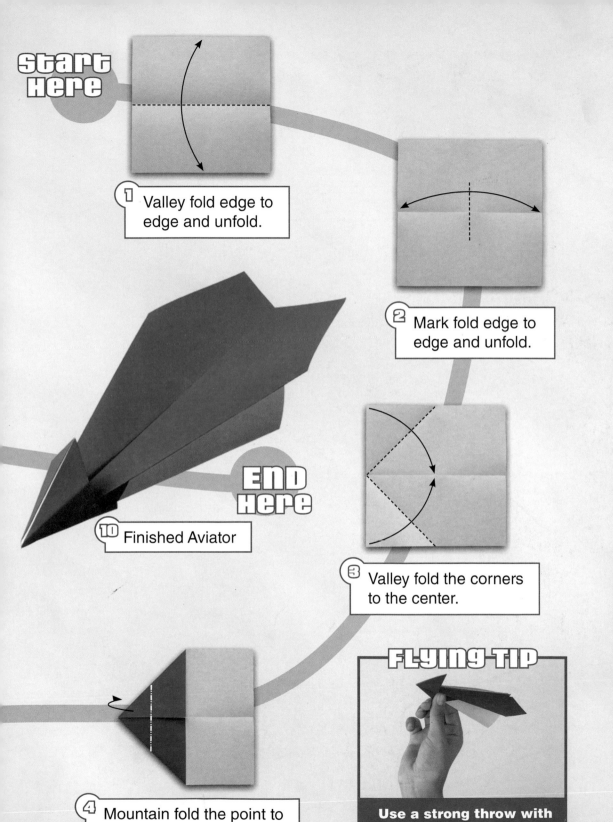

Start HERE

① Valley fold edge to edge and unfold.

② Mark fold edge to edge and unfold.

③ Valley fold the corners to the center.

END HERE

⑩ Finished Aviator

④ Mountain fold the point to the mark made in step 2.

FLYING TIP

Use a strong throw with a slight upward angle.

13

FanG

DESIGNED BY CHRISTOPHER L. HARBO

Tiny teeth give the Fang a dangerous look, but this gentle glider won't bite. The plane's light wings are at the mercy of air currents. In flight, it sways from side to side as it crosses a room.

materials

* 8.5- by 11-inch (22- by 28-cm) paper

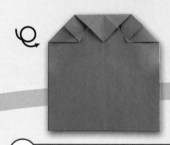

5 Turn the model over.

6 Valley fold the top corners to the center. Allow the tiny flaps behind the corners to release to the top.

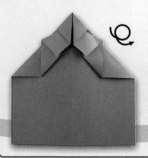

7 Turn the model over.

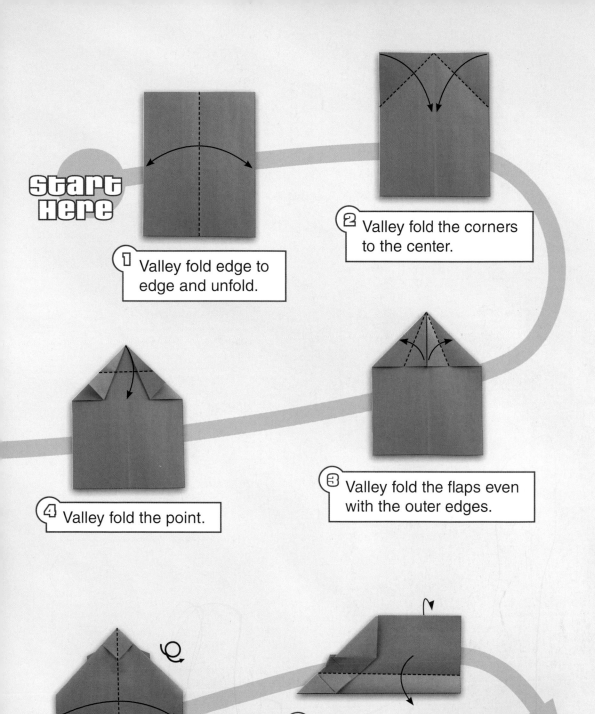

Start Here

1 Valley fold edge to edge and unfold.

2 Valley fold the corners to the center.

3 Valley fold the flaps even with the outer edges.

4 Valley fold the point.

9 Valley fold the top layer. Repeat behind.

8 Valley fold the model in half and rotate.

turn page

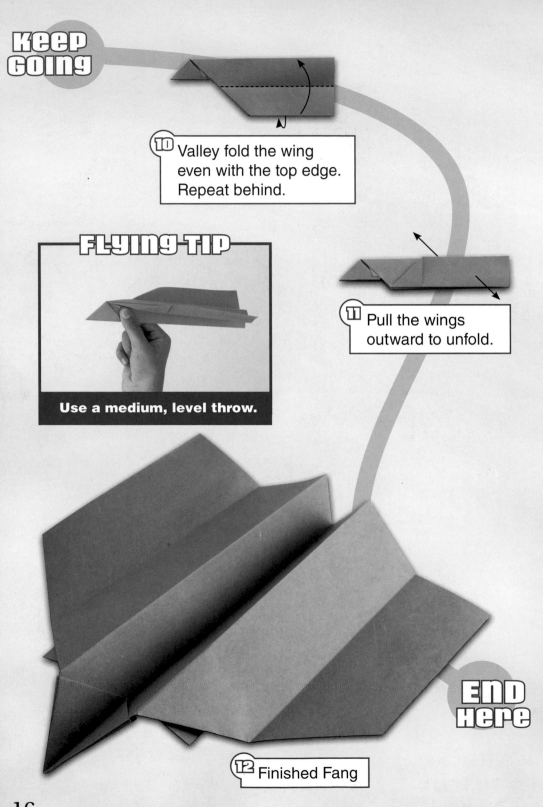

KEEP GOING

10 Valley fold the wing even with the top edge. Repeat behind.

FLYING TIP

Use a medium, level throw.

11 Pull the wings outward to unfold.

END HERE

12 Finished Fang

16

Lazy Lander

DESIGNED BY CHRISTOPHER L. HARBO

Make way for the Lazy Lander! This plane gets its magic from the binder clip. Placed under the nose, the clip gives the glider the weight it needs to fly. Better yet, the clip's legs can serve as landing gear.

materials

* 8.5- by 11-inch (22- by 28-cm) paper
* small binder clip

start here

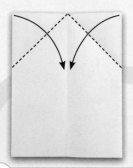

2 Valley fold the corners to the center.

3 Valley fold the point.

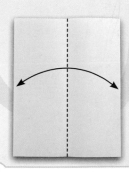

1 Valley fold edge to edge and unfold.

turn page

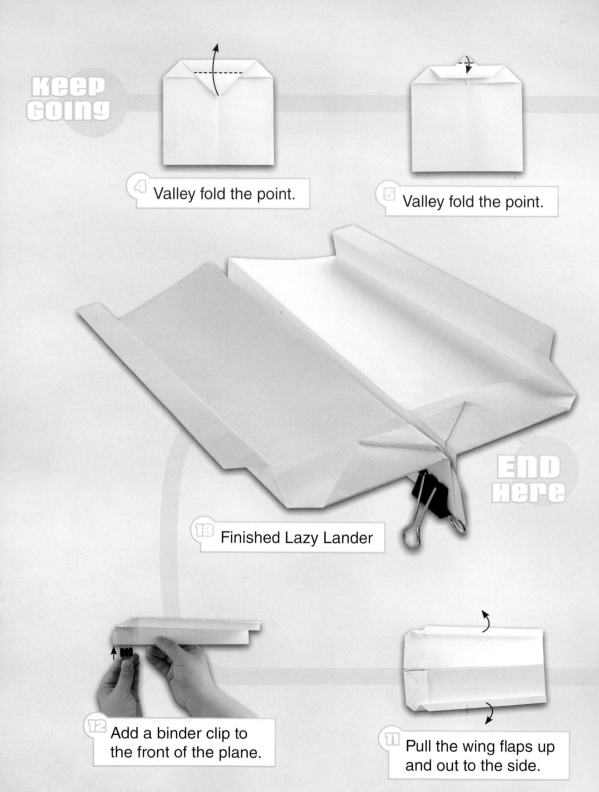

4 Valley fold the point.

5 Valley fold the point.

13 Finished Lazy Lander

12 Add a binder clip to the front of the plane.

11 Pull the wing flaps up and out to the side.

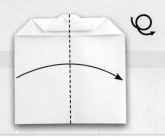

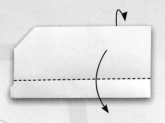

6. Valley fold the model in half and rotate.

7. Valley fold the top layer. Repeat behind.

FLYING TIP

Use a medium, level throw.

8. Valley fold the edge of the wing. Repeat behind.

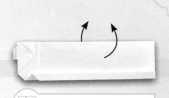

10. Lift the wings.

9. Valley fold the wing flap even with the bottom edge. Repeat behind.

Hang Glider

The Hang Glider takes you soaring to new heights. With the right throw, this glider climbs into the air. When it can go no higher, it banks to the side and curves around the room.

materials

* 10-inch (25-cm) square of paper

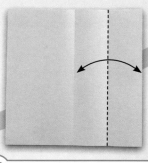

2 Valley fold to the center and unfold.

start Here

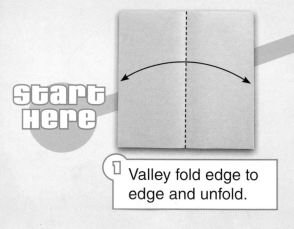

1 Valley fold edge to edge and unfold.

7 Valley fold at A.

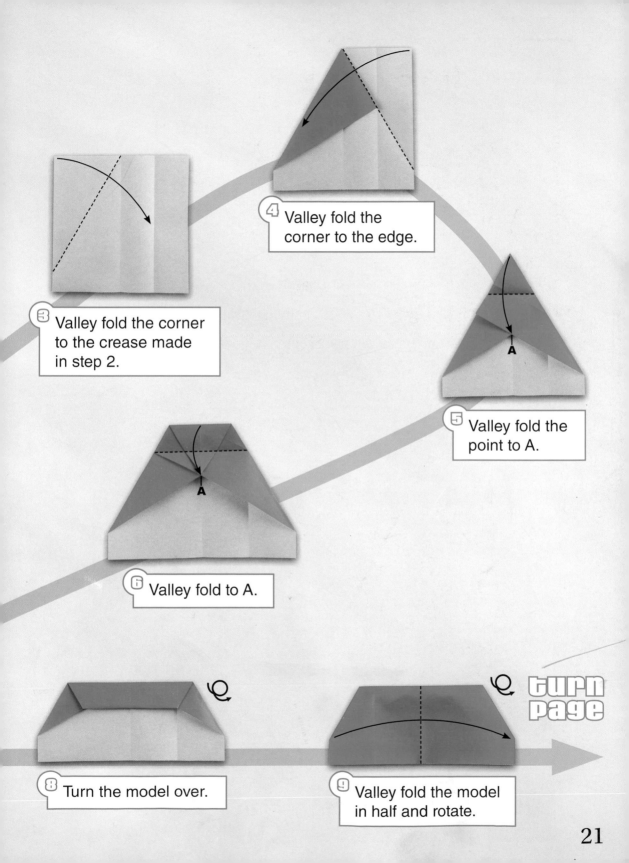

3 Valley fold the corner to the crease made in step 2.

4 Valley fold the corner to the edge.

5 Valley fold the point to A.

6 Valley fold to A.

8 Turn the model over.

9 Valley fold the model in half and rotate.

turn page

21

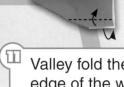

10 Valley fold the top layer. Repeat behind.

11 Valley fold the edge of the wing. Repeat behind.

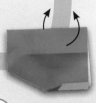

12 Lift the wings.

13 Lift the wing flaps so they stand up at 90-degree angles.

FLYING TIP

END HERE

14 Finished Hang Glider

Use a medium throw with a slight upward angle.

STEADY EDDIE

DESIGNED BY CHRISTOPHER L. HARBO

Get ready for the Steady Eddie. Broad wings and slim wing flaps give this glider a smooth, stable flight. Two small paper clips beside the nose help guide the craft as it comes in for a landing.

materials

* 8.5- by 11-inch (22- by 28-cm) paper
* two small paper clips

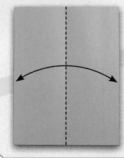

1 Valley fold edge to edge and unfold.

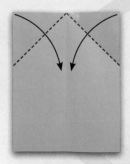

2 Valley fold the corners to the center.

3 Valley fold the point.

turn page

④ Valley fold the point.

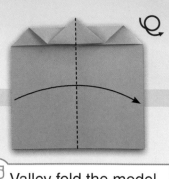

⑤ Valley fold the model in half and rotate.

⑪ Lift the wings.

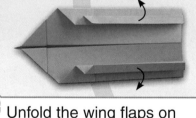

⑩ Valley fold the edge of the wing even with the crease made in step 9. Repeat behind.

⑫ Unfold the wing flaps on the creases made in step 8. Allow the edges of the wings to become L-shaped runners under the wings.

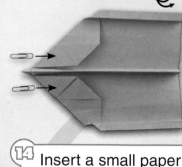

⑭ Insert a small paper clip on each side of the nose. Turn the model over.

⑬ Turn the model over.

24

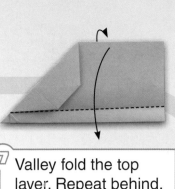

6 Valley fold the left corner. Repeat behind.

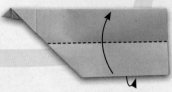

7 Valley fold the top layer. Repeat behind.

9 Valley fold the edge of the wing even with the bottom edge. Repeat behind.

8 Valley fold the edge of the wing even with the top edge. Repeat behind.

END Here

15 Finished Steady Eddie

FLYING TIP

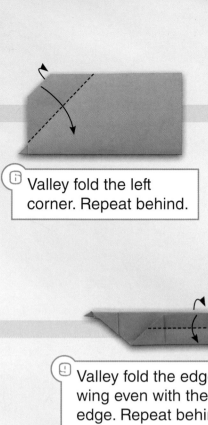

Use a medium throw with a steep upward angle.

D-WING

The D-wing's flight depends on how you release it.
One flight might be long, smooth, and straight.
The next might wobble, curve, and dive. It's a model
that will keep you guessing.

materials

* 8.5- by 11-inch (22- by 28-cm) paper

4 Turn the paper over.

5 Push at point A. Collapse the paper on the existing creases to form a triangle.

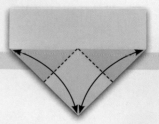

6 Valley fold the top layers to the point and unfold.

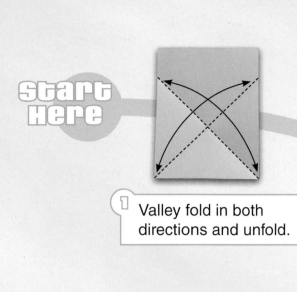

1 Valley fold in both directions and unfold.

2 Turn the paper over.

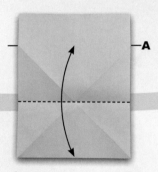

A

3 Valley fold so the corners meet at A and unfold.

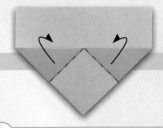

7 Mountain fold the top layers on the creases made in step 6.

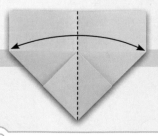

8 Valley fold the model in half and unfold.

turn page

KEEP GOING

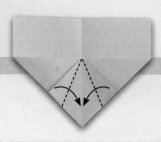

END HERE

9 Valley fold the corners of the top flap to the center.

16 Finished D-wing

15 Lift the wing flaps so they stand up at 90-degree angles.

14 Valley fold the edges of the wings.

28

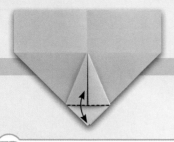

10 Valley fold the point and unfold.

11 Tuck the flaps into the pockets of the point.

FLYING TIP

Pinch the back of the wing with two fingers and your thumb. The model will bend upward in the middle. Release with a strong forward flick of the wrist.

12 Turn the model over.

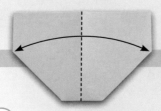

13 Valley fold the model in half and unfold.

Hang Time

How long can you keep a paper airplane in the air? The world record, set by Takuo Toda of Japan, is 27.9 seconds. Challenge a friend to a game of Hang Time to see whose plane can soar the longest.

materials

- large, open room
- stopwatch
- pencil
- notepad
- 2 paper airplanes

What you do

1. Stand in the center of a large, open room.

2. Ask your friend to use a stopwatch to time the flights of your plane. Time begins the instant the plane leaves your hand. Time ends the moment the plane hits the ground.

3. Launch your plane 10 times. Try throwing it with different strengths and angles to achieve the best flight. Write down the flight times for each launch on a notepad.

4. Switch roles with your friend and repeat step 3.

5. Compare the flight times of your plane to your friend's times. The person who has the longest flight is the Hang Time champion.

Read More

Dewar, Andrew. *Fun and Easy Paper Airplanes.* North Clarendon, Vt.: Tuttle Publishing, 2008.

Harbo, Christopher L. *The Kids' Guide to Paper Airplanes.* Kids' Guides. Mankato, Minn.: Capstone Press, 2009.

Schmidt, Steven H. *Sticky Note Paper Airplanes.* New York: Sterling Publishing, 2006.

Internet Sites

FactHound offers a safe, fun way to find Internet sites related to this book. All of the sites on FactHound have been researched by our staff.

Here's all you do:

Visit *www.facthound.com*

Type in this code: 9781429647434

Edge Books are published by Capstone Press,
151 Good Counsel Drive, P.O. Box 669, Mankato, Minnesota 56002.
www.capstonepub.com

 Books published by Capstone Press are manufactured with paper
containing at least 10 percent post-consumer waste.

Library of Congress Cataloging-in-Publication Data
Harbo, Christopher L.
 Paper airplanes, Pilot level 3 / by Christopher L. Harbo.
  p. cm.—(Edge books. Paper airplanes)
 Includes bibliographical references.
 Summary: "Provides instructions and photo-illustrated diagrams for making a
  variety of traditional and original paper airplanes"—Provided by publisher.
 ISBN 978-1-4296-4743-4 (library binding)
 1. Paper airplanes—Juvenile literature. I. Title. II. Series.

 TL778.H3735 2011
 745.592—dc22   2010001006

Editorial Credits
Kyle Grenz, designer; Marcie Spence, media researcher; Marcy Morin, scheduler;
 Laura Manthe, production specialist

Photo Credits
Capstone Studio/Karon Dubke, all planes and steps
Shutterstock/newphotoservice, cover (background); Serg64, cover (background)

Printed in the United States of America in Stevens Point, Wisconsin.
062011   006228WZVMI